Presented to

From

Just Like Jesus Said

Show Each Other

Forgiveness

Illustrations by Susan Reagan

MelodyCarlson

Broadman & Holman Publishers   Nashville, Tennessee

Text copyright ©2002 by Melody Carlson
Illustration copyright ©2002 by Susan Reagan
Cover and interior design: UDG | DesignWorks

Published in 2002 by Broadman & Holman Publishers,
Nashville, Tennessee

LIBRARY OF CONGRESS CATALOGING-IN-PUBLICATION DATA

Carlson, Melody.
Show each other forgiveness / by Melody Carlson ; illustrations by Susan Reagan.
p. cm. -- (Just like Jesus said series)
ISBN 0-8054-2385-0
[1. Forgiveness--Fiction. 2. Behavior--Fiction. 3. Christian life--Fiction.
4. Stories in rhyme.] I. Reagan, Susan, ill. II. Title.

PZ8.3.C19475 Fo 2002
[E]--dc21   2001043317

All rights reserved. Printed in Korea.

ISBN 0-8054-2385-0

2   3   4   5   6   07   06   05   04   03

Show Each Other Forgiveness

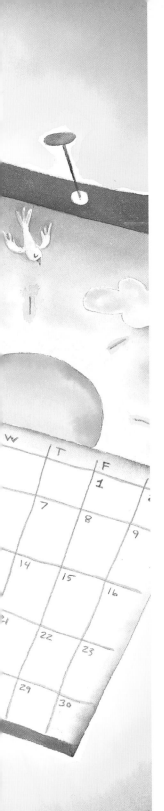

A VERY LONG, long time ago,

I got all kind of freaked.

I had this monstrous problem.

Well, okay, it was last week!

But then I learned a lesson

That makes me stop and think,

Before I get all angry

And make a great, big stink.

The way the whole thing started,

Was my friend, Oliver Small,

While playing in my backyard,

Misplaced my soccer ball.

We searched the whole yard over,

High 'n' low and all around.

But when our search was over,

My ball was never found.

And then I turned to Oliver

And yelled right in his face,

"I thought you were the greatest friend

But you're just a disgrace!

You came to play at my house

And then you loose my toys,

I think that you are hopeless

And the very worst of boys!"

Then Oliver just walked away

His head was hanging down.

He never said, "I'm sorry."

He never made a sound.

And even though I understood

How I'd made my friend sad,

Right at that time, I did not care,

For I was madder than mad!

I wished for a mean vulture

To swoop down and snip his nose!

I wished for a gorilla

To come chew upon his toes!

For all I cared for Oliver

He could be a big balloon,

That floated up above the clouds

And landed on the moon!

15

And while I sat on my front porch

Thinking these mean things,

Amanda Watkins came along

To show me her new rings.

Now I really like Amanda,

For a girl she is all right.

But for some unknown reason

We both began to fight.

I can't even remember

All the crazy words we said.

But I do think that she called me:

"A big, silly, numskull-head."

And that's when I began to yell,

"I wish you'd just get lost.

Go hike up to the North Pole

Where your face will turn to frost!"

My day continued to get worse,

When I discovered Sue,

My pesky, little sister,

(With nothing better to do)

Had trespassed right into my room.

She played with all my stuff.

But I caught her red-handed

And I yelled, "That is enough!"

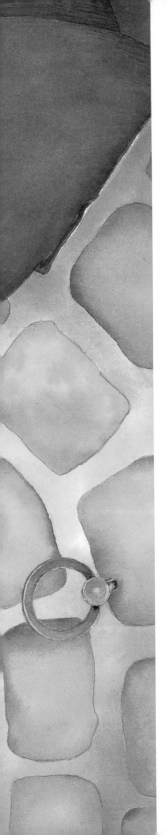

"Stay out of there," I yelled at Sue.

"You sneaky little sneak!

Don't ever step into my room,

Not next year or next week!"

And that's when I wished my sister

Would be kidnapped by wild bears,

And locked into a dungeon

That hadn't any stairs.

23

About that time, my mom stepped in,

She told me not to shout.

She said, "Now go up to your room.

It's time for a *time-out.*"

Well, I stomped loudly up the stairs,

And slammed my door real tight.

There, I would stay forevermore,

At least until the night.

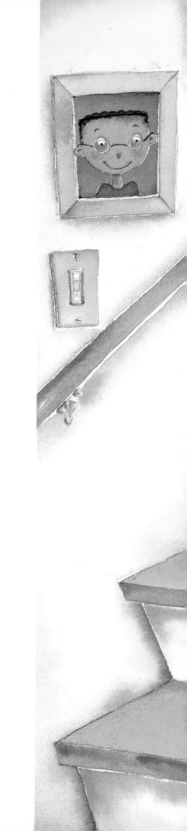

I'd stay in here and starve all night,

For all that anyone cared.

They'd find me sick and shriveled up,

Not that I'd be scared.

And boy, would they be sorry,

When they found me here like this.

That is if anyone bothered

To come for their bedtime kiss.

But as I sat there all alone,

My heart grew very sad.

Could this whole thing be all my fault

Because I got so mad?

And that's when I remembered

What Lord Jesus said to do,

He said, "To forgive others,

Just like I've forgiven you."

I thought about my family, I thought about my friends.

I knew I must forgive them, and that I must make amends.

But first I prayed to Jesus, and I told him I was wrong.

And then my heart grew happy, it didn't take that long.

And after I forgave them all, I knew what I must say.

I said, "I'm sorry," to each one, for all I'd done that day.

And now I understand just why my heart needs to forgive.

It's what love is all about—the best way we can live!

"Do not judge, and you will not be judged.
Do not condemn, and you will not be condemned.
Forgive, and you will be forgiven."

LUKE 6:37